Contents

Some words are printed in bold, **like this**. You can find out what they mean in the glossary. You can also look in the box at the bottom of the page where the word first appears.

HIGH-SPEED WORLD

Speed lovers around the world have found many different ways to go fast! They fly super-fast planes, or race across lakes in boats. They zoom across deserts in cars, or whizz around racetracks on motorbikes. Use this map to find the fastest machines on Earth:

NORTH
AMERICA

PACIFIC
OCEAN

You can find this speed bar at the bottom of every page. It will show you the top speed of all the machines.

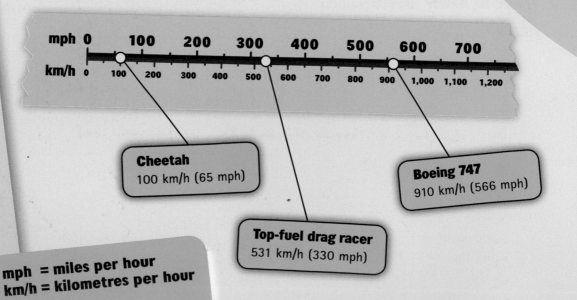

mph 0   100   200   300   400   500   600   700

km/h 0   100   200   300   400   500   600   700   800   900   1,000   1,100   1,200

Cheetah
100 km/h (65 mph)

Boeing 747
910 km/h (566 mph)

Top-fuel drag racer
531 km/h (330 mph)

mph = miles per hour
km/h = kilometres per hour

ATOMIC

PAUL MASON

www.raintreepublishers.co.uk
Visit our website to find out more information about **Raintree** books.

To order:
☎ Phone 44 (0) 1865 888112
▤ Send a fax to 44 (0) 1865 314091
▣ Visit the Raintree bookshop at **www.raintreepublishers.co.uk** to browse our catalogue and order online.

First published in Great Britain by Raintree, Halley Court, Jordan Hill, Oxford OX2 8EJ, part of Harcourt Education. Raintree is a registered trademark of Harcourt Education Ltd.

Editorial: Louise Galpine, Rosie Gordon, Dave Harris, and Stig Vatland
Design: Victoria Bevan and Bigtop
Picture Research: Mica Brancic and Elaine Willis
Production: Camilla Crask

Originated by Chroma Graphics Pte. Ltd
Printed and bound in China by by WKT

10 digit ISBN 1 406 20347 5 (hardback)
13 digit ISBN 978 1 406 20347 9
11 10 09 08 07
10 9 8 7 6 5 4 3 2 1

10 digit ISBN 1 406 20368 8 (paperback)
13 digit ISBN 978 1 4062 0368 4
12 11 10 09 08
10 9 8 7 6 5 4 3 2 1

British Library Cataloguing in Publication Data
Mason, Paul, 1967–
World's fastest machines. – (Atomic)
629'.04
A full catalogue record for this book is available from the British Library.

Acknowledgements
The publishers would like to thank the following for permission to reproduce photographs: American Suzuki Motor Corporation p. **20**; Center for Automotive Research, The Ohio State University p. **16**; Corbis pp. **9** (Philip Wallick), **27** (Louie Psihoyos), **6**, **8**; Corbis/Bettmann p. **7**; Corbis/NASA p. **29**; Corbis/Reuters p. **19** (Gustau Nacarino); Getty Images/Allsport p. **10** (Harry How); Empics/AP p. **13**; Getty Images/Keystone p. **23**; Getty Images/Science Faction p. **26** (Louie Psihoyos); National Archives of Australia p. **22**; Reuters/Juan Medina p. **25**; Rex Features p. **14**. Cover: Corbis (**top**) and Corbis (Zefa/Gary Salter).

The publishers would like to thank Diana Bentley, Nancy Harris, and Dee Reid for their assistance in the preparation of this book.

Every effort has been made to contact copyright holders of any material reproduced in this book. Any omissions will be rectified in subsequent printings if notice is given to the publishers.

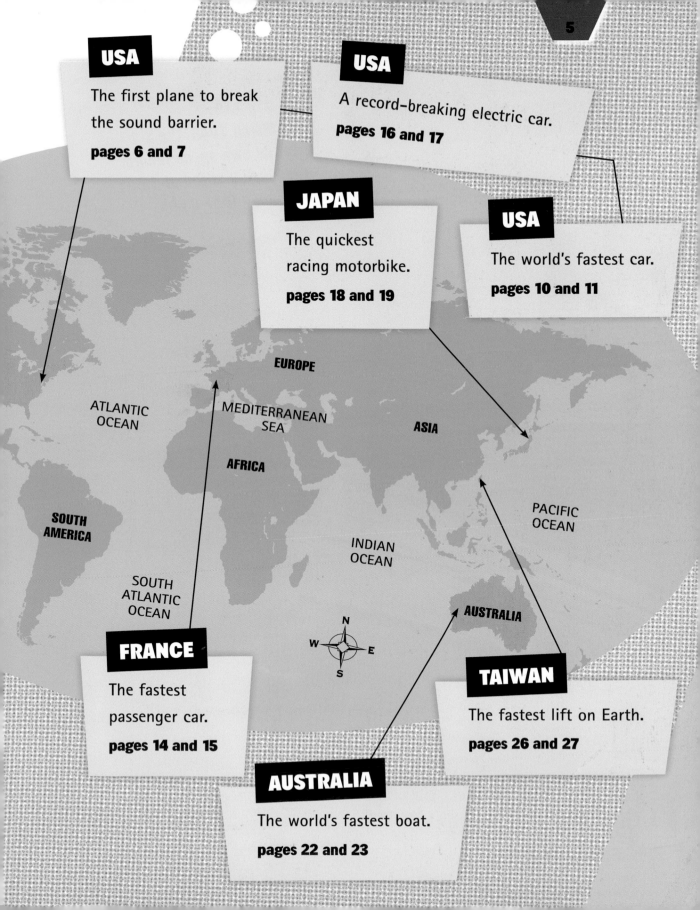

USA

The first plane to break the sound barrier.

pages 6 and 7

USA

A record-breaking electric car.

pages 16 and 17

JAPAN

The quickest racing motorbike.

pages 18 and 19

USA

The world's fastest car.

pages 10 and 11

EUROPE

ATLANTIC OCEAN

MEDITERRANEAN SEA

ASIA

AFRICA

SOUTH AMERICA

PACIFIC OCEAN

INDIAN OCEAN

SOUTH ATLANTIC OCEAN

FRANCE

The fastest passenger car.

pages 14 and 15

N
W E
S

AUSTRALIA

TAIWAN

The fastest lift on Earth.

pages 26 and 27

AUSTRALIA

The world's fastest boat.

pages 22 and 23

Fast fact

In March 1948, the X-1 beat its own speed record. It reached a speed of 1,541 km/h (957 mph).

The X-1's design was based on a bullet, with a long, slim shape.

Top speed!
1,541 km/h (957 mph)

SPEEDBAR

mph	0	100	200	300	400	500	600	700	800	900	1,000	1,100	1,200	1,300	1,400	1,500	1,600	1,700	1,800	1,900	2,000

km/h 0 100 200 300 400 500 600 700 800 900 1,000 1,100 1,200 1,300 1,400 1,500 1,600 1,700 1,800 1,900 2,000 2,100 2,200 2,300 2,400 2,500 2,600 2,700 2,800 2,900 3,000 3,100 3,200 3,200

SUPERSONIC!

On 14 October 1947, for the first time ever, a machine went faster than sound can travel.

Unbreakable

The X-1 aeroplane reached 1,127 km/h (700 mph). Some people had thought it would be impossible for a plane to travel so fast. Other planes had fallen apart at much lower speeds. The X-1's shape was designed to be very **aerodynamic**, so that this would not happen.

NAME: "Chuck" Yeager
BORN: 13/2/23

Yeager was the World War 2 **fighter ace** who flew the X-1 through the **"sound barrier"**.

aerodynamic	able to move through air easily
fighter ace	wartime pilot famous for the number of enemy planes he shot down
sound barrier	speed at which sound travels

THE FASTEST PILOTED PLANE

The fastest ever piloted plane was the Blackbird SR-71. It could travel at 3,530 km/h (2,193 mph).

New York to London

Passenger aeroplanes take about 7 hours to fly from New York to London. The Blackbird could do the same trip in just under 2 hours! But it used so much fuel that it was too expensive to run. It is now only seen in museums.

Blackbird pilots had to wear special suits to protect them because they flew so high in the sky.

instrument panel set of dials and displays. They give a driver or pilot information about speed, temperature, and height, for example.

mph	0	100	200	300	400	500	600	700	800	900	1,000	1,100	1,200	1,300	1400	1,500	1,600	1,700	1,800	1,900	2,00
km/h	0	100	200	300	400	500	600	700	800	900	1,000	1,100	1,200	1,300	1,400	1,500	1,600	1,700	1,800	1,900	2,000	2,100	2,200	2,300	2,400	2,500	2,600	2,700	2,800	2,900	3,000	3,100	3,200

air temperature at 24 km (15 miles): -57 °C (-71 °F)

temperature of front edge of wing: 427 °C (801 °F)

The Blackbird's shape helped it to travel very quickly through the air.

Fast fact

Blackbird pilots did not need to look out of the windows. Instead the instrument panel gave them all the information they needed.

Top speed!
3,530 km/h (2,193 mph)

Thrust SSC speeds across the Black Rock Desert in Nevada, USA.

Fast fact

Thrust's driver used parachutes to slow the car down when he wanted to stop.

Thrust SSC

WEIGHT: 10 tons

LENGTH: 16.5 m (54 feet)

POWER: 110,000 **horsepower**

Top speed!
1,228 km/h (763 mph)

SPEEDBAR

| mph | 0 | 100 | 200 | 300 | 400 | 500 | 600 | 700 | 800 | 900 | 1,000 | 1,100 | 1,200 | 1,300 | 1,400 | 1,500 | 1,600 | 1,700 | 1,800 | 1,900 | 2,000 |

THE FASTEST CAR ON EARTH

In October 1997, a car went faster than the speed of sound for the first time. Its name was Thrust SSC.

A bumpy ride

Thrust reached an **average speed** of 1,228 km/h (763 mph). Driving Thrust must have been very scary. The driver sat between the engines. Thrust's four wheels were made of solid metal. Without any tyres on the wheels, it must have been a bumpy ride!

average speed — in speed trials, the average speed is the top speeds over two attempts added together and then divided by two

horsepower — way of measuring how powerful an engine is. One horsepower was originally supposed to be the same as the pulling power of one horse.

,100 2,200 2,300 2,400 2,500 2,600 2,700 2,800 2,900 3,000   6,000 6,100 6,200 6,300 6,400 6,500 6,600 6,700 6,800 6,900 7,000
3,400 3,500 3,600 3,700 3,800 3,900 4,000 4,100 4,200 4,300 4,400 4,500 4,600 4,700 4,800   9,700 9,800 9,900 10,000 10,100 10,200 10,300 10,400 10,500 10,600 10,700 10,800 10,900 11,000 11,100 11,200

THE FASTEST DRAG RACERS

Top-fuel drag race cars can accelerate faster than almost any other vehicle on Earth.

More power

These incredible machines can reach 160 km/h (100 mph) in less than a second.

Each **cylinder** in a top–fuel racer's engine produces 750 **horsepower**. That's as much as a **Formula One** racecar. Top fuellers have eight cylinders. This means they have eight times the horsepower of a Formula One car!

Fast fact

Top-fuel drag racers can cover 400 metres (0.25 miles), or once around an athletics track, in about 4.5 seconds.

Top speed!
531 km/h (330 mph)

SPEEDBAR

mph	0	100	200	300	400	500	600	700	800	900	1,000	1,100	1,200	1,300	1,400	1,500	1,600	1,700	1,800	1,900	2,00

km/h	0	100	200	300	400	500	600	700	800	900	1,000	1,100	1,200	1,300	1,400	1,500	1,600	1,700	1,800	1,900	2,000	2,100	2,200	2,300	2,400	2,500	2,600	2,700	2,800	2,900	3,000	3,100	3,200	3

A top-fuel drag racer races away from the start line.

accelerate	increase speed or go faster
cylinder	part of the engine that produces power
Formula One	series of high-speed car races that takes place in different countries around the world

2,100 2,200 2,300 2,400 2,500 2,600 2,700 2,800 2,900 3,000   6,000 6,100 6,200 6,300 6,400 6,500 6,600 6,700 6,800 6,900 7,000

3,400 3,500 3,600 3,700 3,800 3,900 4,000 4,100 4,200 4,300 4,400 4,500 4,600 4,700 4,800   9,700 9,800 9,900 10,000 10,100 10,200 10,300 10,400 10,500 10,600 10,700 10,800 10,900 11,000 11,100 11,200

The Bugatti Veyron can cover the length of a football pitch in under a second.

Top speed!
400 km/h (248.5 mph)

SPEEDBAR

| mph | 0 | 100 | 200 | 300 | 400 | 500 | 600 | 700 | 800 | 900 | 1,000 | 1,100 | 1,200 | 1,300 | 1,400 | 1,500 | 1,600 | 1,700 | 1,800 | 1,900 | 2,00 |
| km/h | 0 | 100 | 200 | 300 | 400 | 500 | 600 | 700 | 800 | 900 | 1,000 | 1,100 | 1,200 | 1,300 | 1,400 | 1,500 | 1,600 | 1,700 | 1,800 | 1,900 | 2,000 | 2,100 | 2,200 | 2,300 | 2,400 | 2,500 | 2,600 | 2,700 | 2,800 | 2,900 | 3,000 | 3,100 | 3,200 |

THE FASTEST PASSENGER CAR

The Bugatti Veyron is the fastest passenger car you can buy. It is also the most expensive!

Speed costs!

The Veyron can reach over 400 km/h (248.5 mph). It goes from 0–96 km/h (0–60 mph) in 2.5 seconds. That's about as long as it takes to read this sentence!

Veyrons cost £800,000 each. The fuel costs are very high, too. The Veyron uses up to 5 litres (1.33 gallons) of petrol each minute. Ordinary cars would use up all their fuel in 10 minutes at that rate!

Fast fact

Bugatti say that they will only ever make 300 Veyrons!

2,100 2,200 2,300 2,400 2,500 2,600 2,700 2,800 2,900 3,000   6,000 6,100 6,200 6,300 6,400 6,500 6,600 6,700 6,800 6,900 7,000
3,400 3,500 3,600 3,700 3,800 3,900 4,000 4,100 4,200 4,300 4,400 4,500 4,600 4,700 4,800   9,700 9,800 9,900 10,000 10,100 10,200 10,300 10,400 10,500 10,600 10,700 10,800 10,900 11,000 11,100 11,200

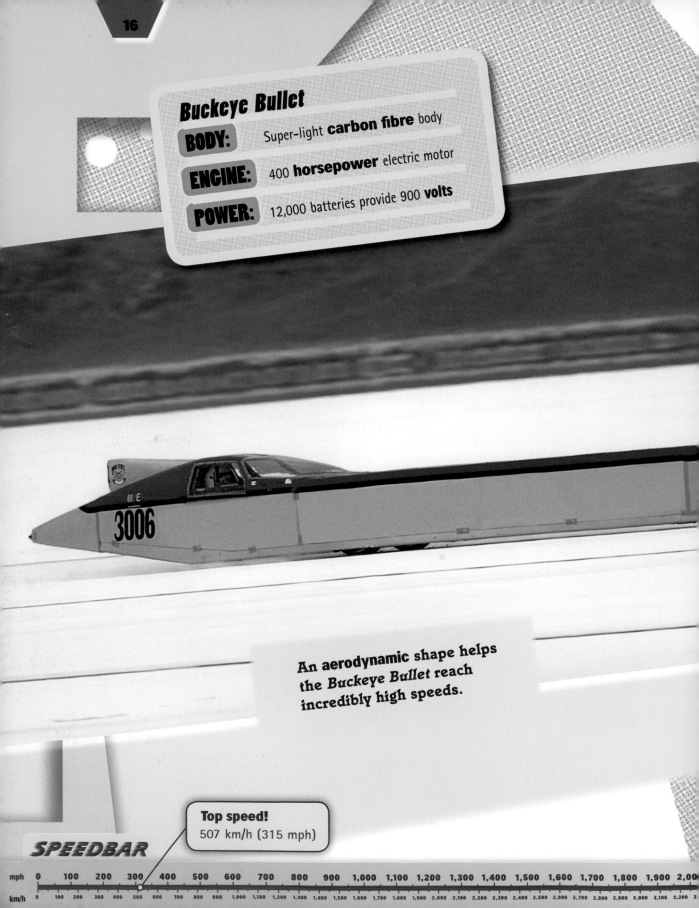

Buckeye Bullet

BODY: Super-light **carbon fibre** body

ENGINE: 400 **horsepower** electric motor

POWER: 12,000 batteries provide 900 **volts**

3006

An aerodynamic shape helps the *Buckeye Bullet* reach incredibly high speeds.

Top speed!
507 km/h (315 mph)

SPEEDBAR

| mph | 0 | 100 | 200 | 300 | 400 | 500 | 600 | 700 | 800 | 900 | 1,000 | 1,100 | 1,200 | 1,300 | 1,400 | 1,500 | 1,600 | 1,700 | 1,800 | 1,900 | 2,000 |

| km/h | 0 | 100 | 200 | 300 | 400 | 500 | 600 | 700 | 800 | 900 | 1,000 | 1,100 | 1,200 | 1,300 | 1,400 | 1,500 | 1,600 | 1,700 | 1,800 | 1,900 | 2,000 | 2,100 | 2,200 | 2,300 | 2,400 | 2,500 | 2,600 | 2,700 | 2,800 | 2,900 | 3,000 | 3,100 | 3,200 |

HIGH-SPEED ELECTRICITY

Not all high-speed cars run on petrol. The *Buckeye Bullet* runs on electricity instead.

Parking problems

Many electric cars are quite slow, but in October 2004, the *Bullet* managed speeds of 507 km/h (315 mph). It used parachutes to slow down.

It may be a record breaker, but this is not an electric car you could take to the supermarket. It is 9.4 metres (31 feet) long, so it would be very hard to park!

carbon fibre	strong and light material made from thin pieces of carbon
volt	measure of how strong electricity is

2,100 2,200 2,300 2,400 2,500 2,600 2,700 2,800 2,900 3,000   6,000 6,100 6,200 6,300 6,400 6,500 6,600 6,700 6,800 6,900 7,000

3,400 3,500 3,600 3,700 3,800 3,900 4,000 4,100 4,200 4,300 4,400 4,500 4,600 4,700 4,800   9,700 9,800 9,900 10,000 10,100 10,200 10,300 10,400 10,500 10,600 10,700 10,800 10,900 11,000 11,100 11,200

THE FASTEST RACE BIKE

The fastest class (type) of motorbike racing is called MotoGP. The fastest MotoGP bike ever is the Honda RC211V. In 2004, racer Alex Barros reached a record 343 km/h (213 mph) on his bike.

RC211V

ENGINE: 990**cc** with 240 **horsepower** – the same power as a sports car

WEIGHT: 150 kg (330 lbs) – about an eighth as much as a sports car

BRAKES: lightweight and powerful **carbon** brakes

EXHAUST: two exhaust pipes, one under the seat

Top speed!
343 km/h (213 mph)

carbon   strong and light material

cc   cubic centimetres. A measure of the size of an engine.

SPEEDBAR

mph	0	100	200	300	400	500	600	700	800	900	1,000	1,100	1,200	1,300	1,400	1,500	1,600	1,700	1,800	1,900	2,0
km/h	0	100	200	300	400	500	600	700	800	900	1,000	1,100	1,200	1,300	1,400	1,500	1,600	1,700	1,800	1,900	2,000	2,100	2,200	2,300	2,400	2,500	2,600	2,700	2,800	2,900	3,000	3,100	3,200

The RC211V is the world's fastest race bike!

Rider tucks behind screen.

Special tyres have extra grip.

Rider tucks behind screen, so the bike and rider are aerodynamic.

The Hayabusa has been the world's fastest bike since 1999.

1298cc engine

aerodynamic shape

Top speed!
300 km/h (186 mph)

SPEEDBAR

mph	0	100	200	300	400	500	600	700	800	900	1,000	1,100	1,200	1,300	1,400	1,500	1,600	1,700	1,800	1,900	2,00
km/h	0	100	200	300	400	500	600	700	800	900	1,000	1,100	1,200	1,300	1,400	1,500	1,600	1,700	1,800	1,900	2,000	2,100	2,200	2,300	2,400	2,500	2,600	2,700	2,800	2,900	3,000	3,100	3,200

THE FASTEST PRODUCTION BIKE

The Hayabusa can reach speeds of 300 km/h (186 mph). It is the fastest production bike (a bike that is for sale in an ordinary motorbike shop) in the world.

Built for speed

The Hayabusa's **aerodynamic** shape means it slips through the air more easily than other bikes. Even the headlight was designed for speed!

The really amazing thing about the Hayabusa is how much it costs. You can buy a new one for less than a family car.

Fast fact

Hayabusa is the Japanese name of a type of falcon.

2,100 2,200 2,300 2,400 2,500 2,600 2,700 2,800 2,900 3,000
3,400 3,500 3,600 3,700 3,800 4,000 4,100 4,200 4,300 4,400 4,500 4,600 4,700 4,800

6,000 6,100 6,200 6,300 6,400 6,500 6,600 6,700 6,800 6,900 7,000
9,700 9,800 9,900 10,000 10,100 10,200 10,300 10,400 10,500 10,600 10,700 10,800 10,900 11,000 11,100 11,200

THE WORLD'S FASTEST BOAT

Amazingly, the record for the world's fastest boat was set almost 30 years ago. Even more surprising is that the boat was built in its owner's back yard!

Breaking the speed limit

Spirit of Australia was built and driven by Ken Warby. It reached an **average speed** of 511 km/h (318 mph). That's over four times the speed limit on a motorway!

Spirit of Australia breaking the water speed record in 1978.

Top speed!
511 km/h (318 mph)

SPEEDBAR

mph	0	100	200	300	400	500	600	700	800	900	1,000	1,100	1,200	1,300	1,400	1,500	1,600	1,700	1,800	1,900	2,00
km/h	0	100	200	300	400	500	600	700	800	900	1,000	1,100	1,200	1,300	1,400	1,500	1,600	1,700	1,800	1,900	2,000	2,100	2,200	2,300	2,400	2,500	2,600	2,700	2,800	2,900	3,000	3,100	3,200

Fast fact

Two people have died trying to break Ken Warby's speed record:

- 1980, Lake Tahoe, Nevada, USA – Lee Taylor died when his £1.46 million boat crashed.
- 1989, Jackson Lake, Florida, USA – Craig Arfons died in a 423 km/h (263 mph) crash.

Ken Warby celebrates his new speed record.

,100 2,200 2,300 2,400 2,500 2,600 2,700 2,800 2,900 3,000   6,000 6,100 6,200 6,300 6,400 6,500 6,600 6,700 6,800 6,900 7,000

3,400 3,500 3,600 3,700 3,800 3,900 4,000 4,100 4,200 4,300 4,400 4,500 4,600 4,700 4,800   9,700 9,800 9,900 10,000 10,100 10,200 10,300 10,400 10,500 10,600 10,700 10,800 10,900 11,000 11,100 11,200

BLOWN AWAY!

The fastest sailing craft in the world is a windsurfer. Over a 500-metre (1,640-foot) course in France, a man called Finian Maynard managed a speed of 48.70 **knots**. That's over 90 km/h (56 mph).

Since 1988, almost every world speed-sailing record has been set on the specially built course at Ste Maries de la Mer, France.

Fast fact

Speed sailing records

YEAR	SAILCRAFT	SPEED (KNOTS)
1993	boat	46.52
2004	windsurfer	46.82
2005	windsurfer	48.70

Top speed!
90 km/h (56 mph)

SPEEDBAR

mph	0	100	200	300	400	500	600	700	800	900	1,000	1,100	1,200	1,300	1,400	1,500	1,600	1,700	1,800	1,900	2,000

km/h 0 100 200 300 400 500 600 700 800 900 1,000 1,100 1,200 1,300 1,400 1,500 1,600 1,700 1,800 1,900 2,000 2,100 2,200 2,300 2,400 2,500 2,600 2,700 2,800 2,900 3,000 3,100 3,200

Harness helps windsurfer to hang on.

$10 \ m^2$ sail has a special shape to "catch" the wind.

Footstraps help windsurfer's feet grip to the board.

Thin, narrow board for speed.

knot   way of measuring speed at sea. One knot is about 1.9 km/h (1.2 mph).

2,100 2,200 2,300 2,400 2,500 2,600 2,700 2,800 2,900 3,000   6,000 6,100 6,200 6,300 6,400 6,500 6,600 6,700 6,800 6,900 7,000
3,400 3,500 3,600 3,700 3,800 3,900 4,000 4,100 4,200 4,300 4,400 4,500 4,600 4,700 4,800   9,700 9,800 9,900 10,000 10,100 10,200 10,300 10,400 10,500 10,600 10,700 10,800 10,900 11,000 11,100 11,200

Fast fact

Each lift cost over £1 million to make!

The Taipei 101 building in Taiwan is the world's tallest building.

Top speed!
61 km/h (38 mph)

SPEEDBAR

mph	0	100	200	300	400	500	600	700	800	900	1,000	1,100	1,200	1,300	1,400	1,500	1,600	1,700	1,800	1,900	2,000

km/h 0 100 200 300 400 500 600 700 800 900 1,000 1,100 1,200 1,300 1,400 1,500 1,600 1,700 1,800 1,900 2,000 2,100 2,200 2,300 2,400 2,500 2,600 2,700 2,800 2,900 3,000 3,100 3,200 3,

THE WORLD'S FASTEST LIFT

How fast could the world's fastest lift be? Pretty fast: it races upwards faster than a car driving through town!

Lift-off!

The fastest lift is in the Taipei 101 building in Taiwan. The lift rises at 1,010 metres (3,314 feet) per minute.

The lift is very well **soundproofed**. The inside of the lift has special tiles and a special floor (see below). On the outside is a noise-reducing cover. There is less noise inside than in most cars travelling at the same speed.

soundproofed   **designed not to let noise in or out**

,100 2,200 2,300 2,400 2,500 2,600 2,700 2,800 2,900 3,000   6,000 6,100 6,200 6,300 6,400 6,500 6,600 6,700 6,800 6,900 7,000

3,400 3,500 3,600 3,700 3,800 3,900 4,000 4,100 4,200 4,300 4,400 4,500 4,600 4,700 4,800   9,700 9,800 9,900 10,000 10,100 10,200 10,300 10,400 10,500 10,600 10,700 10,800 10,900 11,000 11,100 11,200

The Fastest Vehicle on Earth

Our final machine is the fastest vehicle on Earth. The X-43A **unmanned**, radio-controlled aeroplane has reached almost 11,265 km/h (7,000 mph). That is too fast to follow with the **naked eye**.

A new kind of engine

The X–43A uses rockets to **launch** from a bigger plane. But its real speed comes from its "scramjet" engine. The scramjet forces air very quickly through its engine.

If scramjet engines could be used on passenger planes, you could fly anywhere in the world within 90 minutes.

launch | to set off from something
naked eye | the eye without the help of binoculars or cameras
unmanned | not driven by a human pilot

SPEEDBAR

mph	0	100	200	300	400	500	600	700	800	900	1,000	1,100	1,200	1,300	1,400	1,500	1,600	1,700	1,800	1,900	2,00

km/h	0	100	200	300	400	500	600	700	800	900	1,000	1,100	1,200	1,300	1,400	1,500	1,600	1,700	1,800	1,900	2,000	2,100	2,200	2,300	2,400	2,500	2,600	2,700	2,800	2,900	3,000	3,100	3,200

NASA 1 **X-43A**

At top speed, this photo would be impossible to take.

Fast fact

The X-43A is only 3.7 meters (12 feet) long.

Top speed!
11,265 km/h (7,000 mph)

,100 2,200 2,300 2,400 2,500 2,600 2,700 2,800 2,900 3,000

3,400 3,500 3,600 3,700 3,800 3,900 4,000 4,100 4,200 4,300 4,400 4,500 4,600 4,700 4,800

6,000 6,100 6,200 6,300 6,400 6,500 6,600 6,700 6,800 6,900 7,000

9,700 9,800 9,900 10,000 10,100 10,200 10,300 10,400 10,500 10,600 10,700 10,800 10,900 11,000 11,100 11,200

Glossary

accelerate increase speed or go faster

aerodynamic able to move through air easily

average speed in speed trials, the average speed is the top speeds over two attempts added together and then divided by two

carbon strong and light material

carbon fibre strong and light material made from thin pieces of carbon

cc cubic centimetres. A measure of the size of an engine.

cylinder part of the engine that produces power

fighter ace wartime pilot famous for the number of enemy planes he shot down

Formula One series of high-speed car races that takes place in different countries around the world

horsepower way of measuring how powerful an engine is. One horsepower was originally supposed to be the same as the pulling power of one horse.

instrument panel set of dials and displays. They give a driver or pilot information about speed, temperature, and height, for example.

knot way of measuring speed at sea. One knot is about 1.9 km/h (1.2 mph).

launch to set off from something

naked eye the eye without the help of binoculars or cameras

sound barrier speed at which sound travels. The speed varies depending on height above sea level.

soundproofed designed not to let noise in or out

unmanned not driven by a human pilot

volt measure of how strong electricity is

Want to know more?

Books

* *Look Inside Machines: Racing Cars*, Jon Richards (Stargazer Books, 2004)

* *Racing Cars*, David Jefferis (Raintree, 2004)

* *Wild About Planes*, Bill Gunston and David Kimber (Ticktock Media, 2003)

* *Wild About Superbikes*, Bill Gunston and David Kimber (Ticktock Media, 2003)

* *World's Greatest: Motorbikes*, Ian Graham (Raintree, 2005)

Websites

* www.landspeed.com/learn.asp
  This site has lots of information about land speed records.

* www.sciencemuseum.org.uk/
  Here you can find online exhibitions about all sorts of science subjects.

* www.speedace.info/
  This site has information about record-breaking electric cars.

If you liked this Atomic book, why don't you try these...?

Index

Notes for adults

Use the following questions to guide children towards identifying features of report text:

Can you find an example of a general opening classification on page 7?

Can you give an example of a generic participant on page 12?

Can you find examples of non-chronological language on page 15?

Can you find examples of the details of a machine on page 18?

Can you give examples of present tense language on page 21?